Reflections

Poetic Thoughts About **Parkinson's**, **Pandemic & Life**

MARK COXE

Cover Design by Mark Coxe
Cover Photograph by Robert Copeland
Book Design by Mark Coxe & Charles Small
Illustrations Copyright © 2021 Tom C. Murray OBE

Dedicated to my family for putting up with me.

Independently Published by Mark Coxe

Produced with the kind assistance of
Eden Consultancy Group: Design, Print, Web & Marketing

Printed in Great Britain

ISBN: 978-1-5272-9012-9

This book of verse has been written by someone who hated poetry at school, disliked poetry as an adult, but woke up one morning during the 2020 Pandemic with words in his head trying to organise themselves into poems.

All proceeds from the sales of this book will go to Parkinson's UK Scotland Active Appeal and the author's local support group in Fife.

"Adapting to life living with Parkinson's for most people can only be imagined. Living with this life changing condition combined with the last year of COVID-19 has been a huge challenge for everyone in the Parkinson's community.

Mark's poems have brought smiles and cheer throughout the year so it is wonderful to see them all together. These poems tell stories of life, living in the pandemic and how important the work of Parkinson's UK is in bringing people together, sharing, laughing but most of all beating the condition."

Annie Macleod
Scotland Director
Parkinson's UK

"Parkinson's freezes the facial muscles and makes it hard to smile - but I grinned all the way through this terrific collection. Mark tells it like it is and somehow brings the lightest of touches to even the darkest of moments. I look forward to what he does next, which I hope is send me a big bar of dairy milk chocolate." - **Paul Mayhew-Archer** MBE

Paul is the co-writer of "The Vicar of Dibley" and many more comedy shows. He also adapted Roald Dahl's book, "Esio Trot", with Richard Curtis for the BBC.

Since his diagnosis with Parkinson's, he's made a documentary "Parkinson's: The Funny Side" and toured the country with a stand-up comedy show "Incurable Optimist."

He also admits to being a self-confessed chocolate addict!

Paul, if you like a lot of chocolate on your biscuit join our club!

Acknowledgements

Thanks to:

Charles Small for editing the book and giving the author support and encouragement

Tom C. Murray OBE for his excellent illustrations

Robert Copeland for his inspiring Cover Photograph

Rose O'Connor and Eden Consultancy Group for their help and generosity undertaking and financing design, artwork and pre-press

Parkinson's Fife Branch for its support and for financing the project printing

Contents

Ode to the Prom Dress

There is a lonely prom dress,
Hanging limply on the door,
Will it wait forever,
Never to be worn?

Will it ever grace the young girl,
If into the dress she slips,
Or will it be redundant,
Because she's scoffed too many chips?

Last year of school has ended,
It's been lost in a trice,
No more dreadful homework,
Or the chance to catch head lice.

No silly string, no shirts defaced,
No teachers thanked or scorned,
No excitement for the milestone passed,
The school's shut up forlorn.

It's the little things you'll surely miss,
That you never knew you'd had,
A year to never celebrate,
Their final year, that's sad.

So what comes next? Why does the dress
Hold memories of the past?
While also promising future dreams
And friendships which might last.

The answers we might never know,
But the gown and you must part,
As into life you step in style,
Just keep it safely in your heart.

Murder Meal

'It's beans on toast again tonight'
She said with much aplomb,
The expression on his face was like
She'd dropped an atom bomb.

'We cannot leave the house.' said she
'We'll catch Covid 19.'
His reply, to lift a flabby cheek
And gun salute the Queen.

Police called to the disturbance
Had to batter down the door
With hands around each other's necks
They were found on the kitchen floor.

The rozzer's found the pair quite dead
And the cause of the to-do?
Deep within the kitchen cupboard
Was a tin of Campbell's stew.

The atmosphere inside the house
A knife could almost sever,
It was not the situation
But the beans that caused the bother.

The colour of the ceiling
Stated in the police report
Was like that of an eighty's pub
Or at least the policeman thought.

You see the hapless couple
Saw pandemic coming near
So stockpiled loads of baked beans
And frozen bread and beer.

They aimed to isolate themselves
And through greediness and fear
They cleared the shelves of tins of beans
Leaving supermarkets bare.

Their intention was to isolate,
A cunning plan they thought,
But it didn't quite work out like that
Was the official police report.

'T'was the beans that broke the camel's back'
The police report did say,
The monotony of the same old dish
Plus the smell that came their way.

You see the thing that got to them
Was not the deadly virus,
But the effect of eating those baked beans
With consequences disastrous.

Let this be a tale of caution,
The lesson learnt quite clear,
Next time that a pandemic looms,
Don't empty shelves in fear.

But if you are sorely tempted
To supermarket sweep,
Make sure you have variety
Or dire consequences reap.

Mind Over Matter

"What doesn't kill you makes you stronger",
That's what they say to me,
Try living with my Parkinson's,
You'll see that's a fallacy.

Now wait there just a minute!
I should not begrudge my lot,
I may have Parkinson's disease,
But look at the friends I've got.

There's Fife Group just for starters,
(Other branches do exist),
And then there's Parkinson's UK,
Got to add them to the list.

There's lots of splendid people
Who have got the Parki bug,
And live their lives the best they can,
Don't appear to give a shrug.

So if you've seen the Doctor,
Been told Parkinson's your lot,
Join Fife Group* after lockdown,
Good friends out there you've got.

*Look up **https://www.parkinsons.org.uk/information-and-support/
local-groups** to find your local group.

My Friend the Bully

I've met someone who's changed my life,
Mr Parkinson's his name,
He's got lots of different strategies,
My life's not been the same.

He wakes me in the dead of night,
And shakes me till I ache,
I wonder what gives him the right,
To spoil my slumber break.

He sometimes makes me sound quite drunk,
But never buys a pint,
He also makes me stagger,
Makes me really look a sight,

There's other ways he picks on me,
He messes with my mind,
He makes me tend to forget things,
My keys I cannot find.

There's over forty ways he plays,
His games you cannot choose,
Whichever ones he gives to you,
Ultimately you lose.

It took its time to settle in,
It's Parkinson's I've got,
He's not a bully but a friend,
I like him quite a lot.

He's led me to some people,
Who all get bullied too,
They're really rather splendid,
Fife Branch* is there for you.

KEEP CALM

AND JOIN

*PARKINSON'S UK

FIFE BRANCH

We're all in it together,
They keep on telling me.
We'll beat this thing with research,
We will beat it finally.

However in the meantime,
We'll make the most of it,
And as for Mr Parkinson,
You really are a git.

Dry Cough

I have a dry persistent cough,
I've had for many years,
'It's my Parki medication'
I tell anyone that hears.

It's good for social distancing
In a whopping shopping queue,
I always tend to get some space,
But loads of criticism too.

'It's my Parki medication'
I always answer back,
'It's my Parki medication'
It says so on the pack.

Resagaline or Sinemet,
It doesn't bother them,
They hear the cough and that's enough,
They're convinced I'll Covid them.

So when I have a splutter,
I try my best to hide it,
I do it through my nose but then
It's worse, there's no denying it.

'Cos then I just start choking
Which the queue cannot ignore,
And my wife gets so embarrassed
Waiting for my big encore.

I really don't know what to do,
The meds I can't stop taking,
'Cos if I do the effect will be
To exacerbate my shaking.

The only course of action
Is to stay at home and cough,
My wife'll have to do the shop,
She's got the bags, she's off!

Survivor

I have been adrift since Christmas
Floating on my little raft
My boat went down in the South China Sea
Pure luck to find a craft.

My prayer's been answered. I've been saved
My rescue's undisputed
He's a real nice guy but has the look
Of someone persecuted.

He really is a good guy,
To save me from my raft,
I really have been lonely,
I was slowly going daft.

The only trouble with this chap,
He's looking kinda rough,
He's always sweating buckets,
And has a dry, persistent cough.

He mumbles softly all the time,
And I just can't make it out,
It's something he calls Covid,
But it's nowt to care about!

Bone Dry

The problem is my willpower,
Worthy of a proclamation,
Almost everything I can resist
Except of course temptation.

I've run completely out of wine,
I've drunk the whole house dry,
I don't know what I'm going to do,
"Go and shop." I hear you cry.

The trouble is this diktat,
From our Government so dear,
Is wine essential shopping?
In this household "Yes, No Fear!"

With vino my trolley's bulging
Forget the loo roll or dry pasta,
Although wine is not deemed essential
It makes lockdown pass much faster.

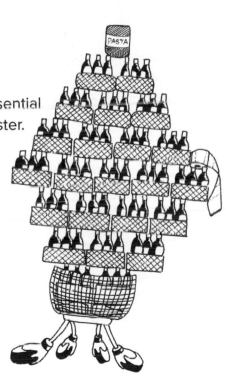

Driven to Exercise

For all those taking exercise
That normally don't bother,
Please listen to this good advice
From one bloke to another.

To all those out there running
On the pavement far too close,
To maintain your social distance,
Don't step out into the road.

For if you do you run the risk
Of causing me to brake,
And if my reaction time's too slow,
We'll collide, for goodness sake.

You'll be bouncing off my bonnet
With all that will entail,
Your face will dent the bodywork
Then through the air you'll sail.

Apart from that you'll run the risk,
The distance rule's been broken,
But rest assured I'll be alright,
If that is any token.

The famous Boy Scout mantra,
'Be prepared.' is mine as well,
Tape measure at the ready,
I will approach, so I can tell.

Would we pass the social distance test
From steering wheel to bumper?
Would we be within the Covid rules
Or would we both be in real bother?

Oh what a joy, it's telling me,
It's under seven feet,
That's such good news, we've passed the test
As you lie crumpled in the street.

So have some consideration
For the guy behind the wheel,
Don't step into the road in haste
And dent his automobile.

I'm alright, I am the driver,
Even though I'm badly shaken,
I'm safe within the knowledge
That Social Distance rules weren't broken.

Westminster's Latest Announcement...

Westminster's proclamation,
Urging us to stay alert,
So we can save our nation,
This deadly virus to subvert.

What's this Boris, don't you know?
Another catch phrase from your lips,
It's not a prime-time game show,
Now we've really had our chips.

Who coins these catchy phrases
That the ministers repeat?
Do they think they will amaze us?
Take them seriously is a feat.

It ends in pandemonium,
Daily briefings imprecise,
PM Boris at his podium,
Like a fool in paradise.

He's the master of oration,
The consummate extrovert,
His hands hold our salvation,
But only serves to disconcert.

Now are we right to criticise?
Not one better than the rest,
They use it to politicise,
For their party they think best.

Now Nicola's, Scotland's number one,
She knows what she's here for,
She'll stand there at her podium,
And when she leaves Frank gets the door*.

*Thanks to Janey Godley

Life Lesson

I was out one night in Singapore,
It was on a flight stop over,
I only went for one quick drink,
See what the nightlife had to offer.

I was going down this quirky street,
Sampling one bar then another,
When I met a group of local girls,
The type you wouldn't want to meet your mother!

There was this girl called Jenny,
Who really put me to the test.
She was absolutely stunning,
Stood head and shoulders above the rest.

She laughed at all my stupid jokes,
We were having a great time,
I never thought I'd fall in love,
I really felt she could be mine.

It didn't dawn on me at first
Singapore Slings, far too many,
And when we had a close embrace,
I found out she was John not Jenny.

It was only then I realised,
That she was in fact a bloke,
In my booze-soaked brain it crystallised,
This was not a flipping joke.

The locals called her "Kai Tai"
This was not the news I'd need,
'Cos she had an Adam's Apple,
And she stood up when she peed.

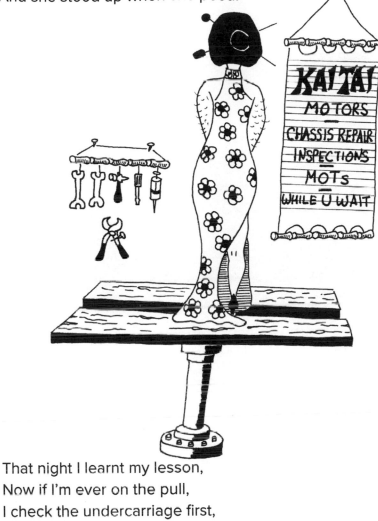

That night I learnt my lesson,
Now if I'm ever on the pull,
I check the undercarriage first,
That's my new found golden rule.

Parki Perv

I used to be a swinger,
Before my Parkinson's attack,
It was really quite a racy time,
In my secluded cul-de-sac.

I'd go to lively parties,
And leave with God knows who,
Get up to lots of capers,
With Anne and Jane and Sue.

But alas all that is finished,
And Parkinson's to blame,
With memory so diminished,
My keys I forget to claim.

They're left there sitting in the bowl,
Which is really quite a shame,
I leave the party all alone,
Parkinson's put out the flame.

And so the Pampas grass out front,
For those that knew the signal,
Is withering and dying back,
Just like my poor libido.

Now Zoom's my interaction,
To my friends I seem forlorn,
If they knew, what's their reaction?
Pants and breeks I've never worn!

So if on any future Zoom chats,
When we regularly assemble,
Be assured I'll always keep it clean,
Keep my hands up on the table.

The Shoe

I saw a shoe on Leven Beach,
And a thought occurred to me,
Just what conclusion would I reach,
Would there be a finder's fee?

What happened to this shoe of leather,
The left foot who knows where?
Certain they should be together,
Sold originally as a pair.

What if the other shoe is on
The foot of someone drowning?
It's not too late for Heaven's sake,
A thought is slowly dawning.

Just wait a tick, what a to do,
I see on close inspection,
'Hong Kong' is marked upon the shoe,
Gives it such a new inflection.

Now that has got me thinking,
This lost and lonely shoe,
If it really came from Hong Kong,
Was the owner Fu-Manchu?

Perhaps it came from Methil,
Or somewhere really far,
From some place quite exotic,
Even somewhere like Dunbar.

Who knows what's really happened?
'Cos the truth is out of reach,
How on a lovely day in June,
It arrived on Leven Beach.

There's No F in Queue

I was in the queue for Sainsbury's,
Stretched a quarter of a mile,
'Twas just before I reached the door,
I noticed something vile.

I'd made a schoolboy error,
A mistake you'd not believe,
I'd left my wallet in the car,
And the queue I'd have to leave!

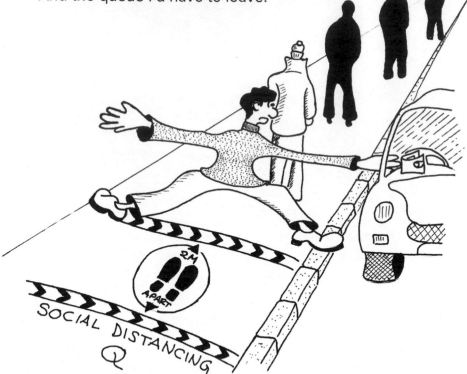

The Protest Protest

It's the inalienable right of everyone,
For thought and word that's free,
That's why our forebears went to war,
To protect democracy.

I respect the right to protest,
On inequality and oppression
But where's your social conscience,
Now's not the time for your opposition.

We all have a bigger obligation,
This life we must protect,
Should keep our social distance,
Or more deaths will take effect.

You can put yourself in danger,
Self-determination is your right,
Just wonder what you're thinking,
When all you want to do is fight.

What happens to the 'R' number,
When you rub shoulders so damn close,
And return to your community,
To the virus you're a host.

So I understand completely,
That you are standing for your rights,
But was it really worth it,
Putting other lives in plight?

Going to the Kirk

Dedicated to Heather Kirk

Heather is a tireless worker,
For Parkinson's UK.
She's volunteered for many years,
So what more can I say?

She's so enthusiastic,
Working wonders for the cause,
She's always full of energy,
Just never seems to pause.

She's often full of new ideas,
To supercharge a meeting,
Her virtual Zoom tea parties,
Well they really take some beating.

They're becoming Scottish legends,
They are really heaps of fun,
But the baking competitions,
Have added inches to my bum!

And as for Heather's quizzes,
The last one was multi choice,
Some of the tennis answers
Were in the questions, oh rejoice!

She's had someone play accordion,
Teuchter music good and loud,
And look who we saw jigging round?
Only oor Annie Macleod!

There's just one thing that bugs me,
Heather lives so far away,
'Cos I'd really like to meet her,
Share a nice wee hug someday.

For now I have to sit and wait,
Just one thought comforts me.
I can always go to see the Kirk,
It's on Zoom – quite virtually!

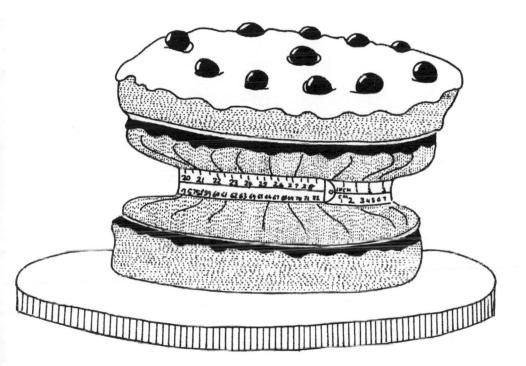

Wish Upon a Virus

The world will never be the same,
That's what they're saying today,
But hasn't that been said before,
When plagues on nations preyed?

Of all the great pandemics,
From Black Death to Spanish Flu,
To victims of Bubonic Plague,
When global panic did ensue.

But will it be so different now,
And will we mend our ways?
Will we ever learn our lesson?
Well that's not what history says.

Because humans are resilient,
And we forget most of our pain,
Look at women during childbirth,
To have another's just insane!

What will we learn from lockdown?
Months of being so introvert,
Not going shopping as a hobby
And buying yet another shirt.

And what of all that plastic,
Wrapping things that we don't need?
Just ends up choking animals,
And fish swimming in the sea.

So has this taught us anything?
Well I think, for what it's worth,
We need to care more for each other
And this planet we call Earth.

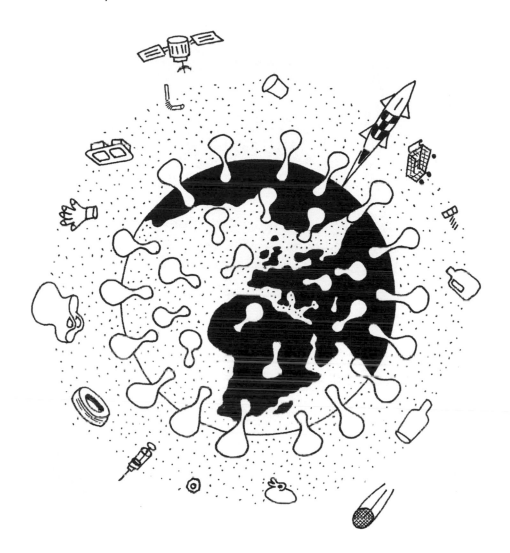

Bed Timing

My kids won't go to sleep at all,
They stay wide awake past ten,
They really seem to have a ball,
I need to use a cage or pen.

I don't know when they'll settle down,
I can't survive till then,
If they don't go to sleep tonight,
I'll have to take up Zen.

They've really got to go to bed,
It's messing with my brain,
I've got to show them who's the boss,
It surely can't be them.

I sometimes get the feeling,
My parenting skills are shoddy.
But then they melt my tired old heart
By dressing like Showaddywaddy!

On the whole my kids are darlings,
It's just when it's time for bed,
I should've stuck with contraception
And got a good night's sleep instead!

Technical Break

My microphone's not working,
It's been playing up for some time,
It looks as if I'm miming,
Which would be an awful crime.

Next time on Zoom if it's not fixed,
A stripy top I'll wear,
And put a beret on my head,
And sit with a glaikit stare.

When someone stops and asks me,
If everything's alright,
I'll put my white gloved hands up,
As if I've had a fright.

I'll do that awful miming thing,
Although it's a proper cliché,
I'm trapped behind a pane of glass,
And I can't get away.

But if you think about it,
It's not that far from real life,
I'm stuck behind a laptop screen,
Or any other Zoom device.

And if you cannot hear me,
At least I can hear you,
I can still enjoy the meeting,
I'm not stuck in Timbuktu!

R N L Why?

It was on a dark and stormy night
And the sea was boiling foam,
The wind was rattling windows,
I was glad I was at home.

It was just before I went to bed,
I glanced out from the landing,
When something briefly caught my eye,
In the place where I was standing.

Was it a distress rocket,
A solitary flare?
It was a brief and glinting light,
I'm sure that it was there.

It was just a millisecond,
And difficult to gauge,
I waited for another one,
For what seemed like an age.

And there it was I'm sure this time,
A flash of red again,
But for the briefest moment,
Through wind and spray and rain.

Quick go and call the Coastguard
There's someone out at sea,
They're praying to be rescued,
Wherever they might be.

The lifeboat crew will scramble,
When the mournful klaxons cry,
And to their sturdy craft they go,
To save a life at sea they'll try.

I stood there rooted to the spot,
Thankful I was not outside,
Trying to keep above the mighty waves,
And all that it implied.

There's the little blip of red again,
But something isn't right,
It's not coming from outside at all,
That tiny red repeating light.

It's only a reflection,
Upon the window pane,
Of the smoke detector warning light,
As the battery starts to wane.

So please call off the lifeboat,
So their lives they will not risk,
It seems upon reflection,
That I was a silly twit.

Sick of This

I live on Baxter Island,
It's a leper colony,
What is this social distancing?
It means bugger all to me.

Parkinson's

Parkinson's is crazy,
Got no reason got no rhyme,
It affects some people awfully,
All down to a small enzyme.

While some get sentimental,
Yearning for what used to be,
Others take what they've been dealt,
With a sigh of 'C'est la vie'.

Some get a rhythmic tremor,
With hands and arms that flick,
It's like strumming on an air guitar,
But without any rock music.

Freezing is also an awful thing,
Soft shoe shuffle in doorways,
While those approaching from behind,
Don't wait for the delays.

As for the medication,
The drugs you have to take,
The side effects creep up on you,
Like a cruel offensive joke.

Here's to all the other symptoms,
Over forty so they say,
And if I was to count them all,
We'd be here all flipping day.

Escaping with Parkinson's

I am in quite a quandary,
It is an awful thing,
The stewardess has given me,
The seat right by the wing.

I'm not needing all that legroom,
I've got Parkinson's Disease,
My leg length doesn't count at all,
But sometimes I can freeze.

Now what if there's a problem,
And the plane crash lands somewhere,
Or ditches in the open sea,
And I can't operate the door?

With people pushing past me,
What would happen if I froze and stopped?
With all that built up pressure,
Through the door I would be popped.

What of those who didn't make it,
Since the queue on Starboard side,
Was caused by someone freezing,
And completely blocked the isle?

If the crash investigation,
Should finger point at me,
I may have Parkinson's disease,
But I have the right to be.

I just sat where I was told to,
By that lovely stewardess,
Who kicked me with her size six shoe,
While I was frozen in distress.

It's not survival of the fittest,
Although of course that's mostly true,
I'll just sit here nice and quietly,
'Cos I've thought the problem through.

British Airways staff receive redundancy notices

07 August 2020

BA Blues

It seems 12,000 pilots,
Are about to lose their jobs,
They work for British Airways,
But they're not elitist snobs.

So just what is a pilot,
And what is it they do?
They're glorified bus drivers,
In the skies they're with the few.

At least if Stagecoach hits the skids,
Bus drivers they don't fuss,
They'll get some more employment,
On a local omnibus.

So what's the pilot gonna do,
His skills he can't transfer,
He doesn't have a PSV,
Of that you can be sure.

And if he was to drive a bus,
You know what he would think,
"We're cruising at low altitude
And this uniform just stinks!"

I really shouldn't slate them,
It's unfair on all those guys,
They always get the brunt of it,
When they fall out of the skies.

The good times that they had were bliss,
They didn't have a clue,
Their jobs would get a viral kiss,
Just see what Covid can do.

The moral of the story,
If you want security,
Don't fly an aero-plane my son,
But drive a bus like me.

UK beaches on red alert after 'unsafe' crowds gather to enjoy 30C heatwave

08 August 2020

What Makes Bournemouth Special?

Why is Bournemouth so appealing
That makes people want to gather
To burn and end up peeling,
In abnormal sunny weather?

The seaside town boasts that it owns,
An impressive iron-made pier,
Seven hundred and seventy-five feet long
Gives you a smile from ear to ear.

The beach is seven sandy miles,
From gritty start to end,
With lots of ice cream parlours,
Designed to make you spend.

The beach is just as sandy,
As others round the coast,
The lifeguards no more randy,
But perhaps they pack the most.

The people come from far and wide,
To enjoy the sandy beach.
All thoughts of Covid gone away,
With the sea within their reach.

They think that herd immunity,
Will protect them from the virus,
But they risk the whole community,
To catch it still quite serious.

Herd immunity's the watch word,
That the politicians covet,
Doesn't mean they have to act like cows,
Or the virus rates won't plummet.

And we'll all remain in lockdown,
Till the end of all our days,
Watching episodes of Countdown,
Dreaming of old holidays.

So what made Bournemouth special?
I really want to know,
Will it be the second highest spike,
Government statistics show?

Lucky Me

I'm just a lucky person,
Just a lucky sort of guy,
Missed disasters by a whisker,
Times when I would surely die.

Like the recent train derailment,
On the national railway line,
I would have been upon that train,
Except in one week's time.

I remember being in Guildford,
A month before the bomb,
In the pub the Guildford four blew up,
Except the police had got it wrong.

I was on a street in London,
But I never got mowed down,
'Cos that maniac Jihadi,
Was in a different part of town.

I could have sailed the seven seas,
And been on the Titanic,
But I wasn't living at the time,
No need for me to panic.

Now I'm really not that lucky,
All these things I might have missed,
I'm a sort of Walter Mitty guy,
Fifty-six and not been kissed.

I'm still living with my parents,
If you could call it that,
They died about six years ago,
But I've kept them in our flat.

I've been picking up their pensions,
Now the police have got involved,
Helping them with their inquiries,
And getting done for benefit fraud.

What DRIG Stands For

The research part of Parkinson's,
Not a thing that floats my boat,
But for fighting Parkinson's, it's the key,
Now it sort of gets my vote.

The Dundee Research Interest Group,
Not an easy one to rhyme,
Now I'm feeling such a nincompoop,
Seems to happen all the time.

The first time that it was mentioned,
I thought they'd said D-Ream,
That 90's pop/rock/dance group,
That almost made girls scream.

What's that to do with Research?
I couldn't understand,
But suddenly I remembered,
Brian Cox was in the band.

A Quantum Physics expert now,
Is Professor Brian Cox.
Pity his work's not Parkinson's.
He's producing programmes for the box.

Even though he's into science,
It surely can't be right,
So I did a search on Google,
And I found with some delight.

That drig's in fact a proper word,
It means something actually,
And it really isn't that absurd,
It's in the Urban Dictionary*.

The entry states quite clearly,
It's a word used by the young,
It means someone who is motherly,
Comforting in any tongue.

Now that's quite coincidental,
For what's really plain to see,
The Research Information Group,
Sounds quite comforting to me.

The coincidences do not end there,
Because the mantra for the team,
Is, "Things can only get better"
Which was a big hit for D-Ream.

*Urban Dictionary

drig Drig is the name of a friendly person who is both intelligent and motherly. They will often make things by hand as gifts, or help out on projects beyond what was expected of them. A drig is someone you can trust and who will make a good friend.

Durdle Don't

There's a tourist spot in Dorset,
On the Jurassic Coast,
That's become a rescue hot spot,
Tourist Boards don't want to boast.

The beach and cliffs at Durdle Door,
Are really quite attractive,
But the undertow just off the shore,
Keeps the rescuers quite active.

This latest little episode,
Saw a swimmer swept to sea,
Into the waves he'd only strode,
To have a little pee.

The little leak became much more,
When he realised with dread,
As he was bobbing off the shore,
Required a number two instead!

He shouldn't eat hot Asian food,
But can't resist a curry,
His favourite one is Vindaloo,
It plays havoc with his tummy.

He thought he'd get away with it,
But when he tried to use the zipper
His wetsuit wouldn't open up,
He would have made a lousy stripper.

T'was the people on the beach who saw
That he was in distress,
And formed a sort of human chain
That reached him with success.

It was only when they got him back
To the golden sand so dry,
That they saw with great displeasure
And they wished they hadn't tried.

And what of other rescues?
I almost hear you ask,
In the past months there's been quite a few,
But none as fragrant as the last.

I suppose the moral of the tale
If there is one, understand,
The sea is not a toilet,
Go dig a big hole in the sand.

Song Sung Blue

The last night of the proms this year,
Isn't going to be the same,
It's nowt to do with Covid,
The do-gooders are to blame.

Rule Britannia won't be blasted out,
By some fat bird with a shield,
Because it mentions slavery,
And that Britain's would not yield.

Are we to blame for what's been done
So many centuries ago?
The times were very different then,
As our history has to show.

By modern standards it is known,
As a crime for all to see,
But they didn't reap what they had sown,
When they made this great country.

It's so wrong that we should denigrate,
Our history that is true,
After all an omelette can't be made,
Unless you break an egg or two.

How far back are we supposed to go,
To rewrite our history,
As far back as the Normans,
In the eleventh century?

Let's not forget the Viking hoards,
And what they used to do,
Rape and pillage was their smorgasbord,
And roll mop herring too.

And what about the Romans,
Who enslaved the local folk,
And made the Ancient Britain's groan,
Under their atrocious yoke?

It's been asked by Monty Python,
What the Romans did for us,
Well, they built some really straight roads,
And some stunning aqueducts.

So, should we dig up Watling Street,
On the M6 Motorway?
Would that give us a new clean sheet,
Make the Romans go away?

So, do us a big favour,
Help us celebrate our past,
And sing each semiquaver,
Like it's going to be our last.

Let's join with that fat lady,
Who's holding spear and shield,
And sing out Rule Britannia,
Beside the toffs who are well heeled.

WTF?

My Martini Girl's teetotal,
Don't have no sex no more,
We used to do it anywhere,
Even on the kitchen floor.

But now the urge has passed her,
The place she'd rather be
Is downstairs watching Netflix,
Than romp upstairs with me.

So what's gone wrong I'm asking,
It shouldn't just be luck,
When I sidle up to her in bed,
And she agrees to have a......

Okay I have put on some weight,
And there's less hair on my head,
But I've got the same old feelings,
You know I'm not completely dead.

So let's both make an effort,
Even if I peak too soon,
You know you're my Martini Girl,
I love you further than the Moon.

Conspiracy Theory

If you are keen on theories
Where governments conspire
Or if there's ever been a cover-up
When a situation's dire

I've got one about a company
An organisation known worldwide
They produce a little blue pill
But that information's classified

They had made the Covid virus
As a sort of PR exercise
But they miscalculated badly
Let their eye's drop from the prize

It all started last November
When their virus was released
Wuhan was the epicentre
And the virus had a feast

It infected many thousands
But the Commie Party State
Kept the outbreak strictly secret
What a big mistake to make

The virus had mutated
When at last China came clean
Now the Pharma Vaccine didn't work
Something they had not foreseen

What made the situation even worse
Was that men succumbed the most
Those with a sexual dysfunction
Caught the virus and were toast

As I've said they make a wee blue pill
For legal reasons can't be named
It's their best and biggest seller
Keeps over fifties in the game

It's for over fifty fatties
Who can't rise to the occasion
With verandas over toy shops
As described by the Aussie nation

They're their main core demographic
And were dropping down like flies
Instead of market leader brand
The soaring 'blueys' sales declined

The execs were in hot water
With the pandemic spread worldwide
The shareholders were disgruntled
With their financial suicide

So they really had to work hard
A brand-new vaccine was produced
To rectify their grave mistake
Demise of 'impotents' reduced

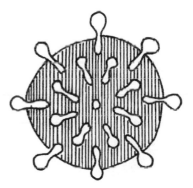

With the whole world celebrating
Blue pill sales went through the roof
Their Q4 target has been smashed
And all I need now is the proof!

Cross Dresser

I'm what's known as a cross dresser,
Have been for many years,
It's something that I live with,
But it can drive me close to tears.

It all started very slowly,
Sort of just crept up on me,
And then finally I realised,
A cross dresser I must be.

It might have started with a sock,
Or a button on a cuff,
But by the time I had got dressed,
I'd really had enough.

I was getting so much slower,
Taking longer by degrees,
And a simple thing like getting dressed,
Would bring me to my knees.

It really was frustrating,
Getting help to put on clothes,
It felt like going back in time,
When mum wiped my runny nose.

What's caused this situation,
This dressing without ease?
A neurological condition,
It's called Parkinson's Disease.

Now there's others on the market,
You don't choose what one you've got,
But it made me a cross dresser,
Bloody furious with my lot!

Bradykinesia

If Parkinson's affects you,
'Body pop' and squirm perchance?
Bet you really don't enjoy it,
'Cos it's not a flipping dance!

If you're freezing in a doorway,
Which can often be quite true,
Don't be taken for that old cliché,
That you've had a drink or two!

It's because of medication,
The result of drugs you pop,
Pills controlling locomotion,
Side effects. 'Just suck it up!'

Dyskinesia's the symptom,
Makes you do this mirthless dance,
Bradykinesia's quite the opposite,
Puts you in a sort of trance.

The good old English language,
Has some great collective nouns,
Some conjure quite an image,
While others just make you frown.

Below are some examples,
I have included here for fun,
Such as women wearing wimples,
Are a superfluidity of nuns.

The collective noun for doggies,
Everyone knows is a pack.
But what about a glaring?
Turns out it's a bunch of cats.

The collective noun for Parkinson's,
For Dyskinesia's obscure,
But for those with Bradykinesia,
It's the Brady Bunch for sure.

Ultimatum

'Just quit your medication.'
My wife has said to me,
She's convinced it's detrimental,
Affects my personality.

I don't know what you're doing,
With all this stupid verse,
But if you do not cut it out,
You'll end up in a hearse.

She's getting quite annoyed now,
Her Scottish brogue quite strong,
But her voice is music to my ears,
Got me breaking into song.

I suppose I'll have to cut it out,
On verse no longer linger,
It's my marriage that I have to save,
Or she'll give me the middle finger.

Glasses

I've lost my flipping glasses,
I'm sure I had them on my nose,
But took them off at some stage,
I kinda just suppose.

Now I just can't seem to find them,
Trouble is without them I can't see,
So what are my flipping chances,
They'll turn up eventually?

It's a blessing that I'm married,
'Cos my wife finds them for me,
But she always treats it like a chore,
And it's done begrudgingly.

It's becoming quite a spectacle,
But I really do not mind,
A spectacle's the next best thing,
When your glasses you can't find.

Out of the Darkness

I'm sorry I've been off the grid,
My mind's a mess with this Covid,
It's not like I've got loads of issues,
I'll not be blubbing into tissues.

But little things keep piling up,
Like quicksand's grip that starts to suck,
Can't shake off this dark reverie,
Churchill's 'Black Dog' has got hold of me.

I need to pull myself together,
Or I'll go under, gone forever,
Into the maelstrom I'll be pulled,
My sense of desolation's fuelled.

I'm not alone, in this I know,
These are strange times, just goes to show,
That when you see a cheeky chappie,
Under his skin he's not so happy.

This virus hasn't got me yet,
I'll fight this feeling you can bet,
And come out on the other side,
Of that I'm sure, like time and tide.

I've had some issues I suppose,
Before this lockdown was imposed,
And I've been quite okay with them,
It's just this virus ain't the same.

At least with things that you can see,
The things that take control of me,
I have a chance of fighting back,
My hands-on wheel, get back on track.

I'm sorry for this frightful dirge,
But my demons I am trying to purge,
A problem shared is surely halved,
Share it some more it's nearly solved.

Dilute enough like orange squash,
This awful mood I'll start to quash,
I won't be feeling down and blue,
I've got my health........
....................That's not quite true!

Cabinet Capers

The government resembles,
A Brian Rix slapstick farce,
Starting with Boris Johnson,
Who sounds like quite an arse.

Matt Hancock comes close second,
It's almost by a nose,
He's like his namesake Tony,
And his ha-ha-half-hour shows.

Now Rishi Sunack's done his best,
Wants the economy to flourish,
He's opened bars and restaurants,
Only the pandemic he has nourished.

Next up is Baroness Evans,
Better known as, 'What's her face'
Since no one's ever heard of her,
Until she cocked up 'Track and Trace'.

On Michael Gove you can rely,
He's the only one with vision,
He'll stab his colleagues in the back,
Number 10 is his ambition.

Sweet Priti Patel's in politics,
To keep the Tory chin up,
What is it that she wants to be?
It's a right-wing party pinup!

Liz Truss is just incompetent,
She's the one who's sorting Brexit,
Not filling me with confidence,
Couldn't find a tunnel exit.

Now the worry that I'm feeling,
How did we vote for all these fools?
They're really not a Cabinet,
Just a box of useless tools!

Sign of the Times

We took the dog to Craigtoun Park
To give him a little run,
But Covid Regs really soured the lark
And took away our fun.

It's that bloody social distancing
And the signs that do declare,
You're to keep six feet from everything
Or two metres to be fair.

Their signs just aren't the ticket
For the guys that use the loo,
The urinal's a small target
From one metre, far less two!

Now maybe twenty years ago
It could have been achieved,
Would have been done with gusto,
Decades later I'm aggrieved.

A picture I don't have to draw
Or frustration have to vent,
On the state of the gents toilet floor
Where my bladder contents went.

Ultimate Test

They've thought of a solution,
To help the failing Track and Trace,
And they really are excited,
It's gonna save the human race.

It's from the Middle Ages,
A procedure tried-and-true,
It's a take on the old ducking stool,
Used to find a witch or two.

To test you for the virus,
They'll strap you in a chair,
And duck you under water,
Use an app so that it's fair.

Now if you can last five minutes,
You're a virus case it's clear,
But if you've drowned that's good news
You're clear of Covid, they'll declare.

We must look on the bright side,
The Government tells us,
They're saving loads on furlough,
And free travel on the bus.

If you're living near a duck pond,
Make the ducklings lose their homes,
And bulldoze the shit out of it,
Before a Test Place it becomes.

For Fox Sake

It's gone three in the morning
Good old British Summer Time
And I'm sitting on my sofa
Writing this here silly rhyme.

I've signed up for a fun run
A misnomer any day
Fun and run just do not mix
Not in my mind anyway.

It's raising funds for Parkinson's
But not in the UK
It's for the MJ Fox Foundation
And they'll be running in LA.

Maybe not in this pandemic year
It is virtual you see
There won't be a big meeting
We'll run individually.

The major issue that I've got
Is my ankle is quite sore
I've hurt my Achilles tendon
Which is really such a bore.

But I think I've a solution
I'll use my bike to get me there
And I'll cycle twice the distance
Plus a bit more to be fair.

It's not the same I realise
But beggars can't be choosers
If I didn't make the effort
Parkinson's would be the losers.

I'm not saying I've raised a fortune
But every dollar counts
We'll know we've helped to find a cure
Which one day they'll announce.

A Comedy of Errors

Is there anybody out there
In a maudlin mood like me,
Who thinks of ways to end it all,
More than just occasionally?

Have you ever thought of driving
Without your seatbelt on
And swerve to hit a bridge support?
Now that doesn't sound like fun.

What if my poor old mangled car
Were to cause a fatal crash
If it bounced into the road again?
I just couldn't live with that.

What if I didn't die outright,
But was pinned there wracked in pain?
No time for second thoughts my lad,
Life would never be the same.

What if I took my medication?
My prescription's nearly due,
Take all the pills together,
With some whisky, ought to do.

But my fingers don't work half as well.
I've got to face the fact,
I'd be dead before I'd got the pills
Out of the blister pack.

Now don't be getting worried
About my mixed-up mental state,
I'm not going to commit suicide,
Not today at any rate.

I suppose it's down to Parkinson's,
This maudlin melancholy mood,
It's really just a passing phase,
I'll continue with the feud.

So, if you're feeling suicidal,
Don't do it! Join my gang.
There'll always be a better day,
Parkinson's can go and hang.

To E or Not to E?

Dedicated to Janet Kerr PWP & Cycle Path Enthusiast

The virtue of an e-bike
It gets you from a to b
It helps you tackle steepish hills
As any fool can see.

But is it really kosher
To put a motor on a bike?
Does it mean you are a cheater
Someone who's not sportsmanlike?

The very first invention
Which these days we call the bike
Was designed in 1881
And was like a sit-on trike.

The rider used to run along
Whilst sitting on the saddle
It had no gears or rubber tyres
You couldn't even pedal.

So why the history lesson?
It's to show how far we've come
Should we listen to the purists
Let them take away our fun?

The inventor Karl Von Drais
Wouldn't recognise his toy
It's got gears and brakes and batteries
Just imagine his great joy.

So what's so bad with e-bikes
If they help us exercise?
Tell the purists that it's progress
As you look them in the eyes.

And as for all those purists
Instead of 'On yer bike'
Let's just keep it pure and simple
And tell them to 'Take a hike'.

Not as Good as it Looks

There's something really magical
When you're anchored out at sea
When it's dark and still and I can see
The shore lights calling me.

It doesn't matter where you are
On some far-flung foreign coast
To see those scintillating lights
Is the sight I love the most.

They look so damned inviting
After many weeks at sea
With nothing to light up the night
But the moon and galaxies.

Perhaps, after all the nights on watch
Of searching for a light
To see so many strung out there
Is a very welcome sight.

Depending on how close you're in
And the climate I suppose
And with a gentle off-shore breeze
Spicy scents assault your nose.

Whatever place you're anchored off
At this distance from the beach
You don't see the degradation
And the problems it's unleashed.

It's not until you get ashore
That you see the locals' plight
You know you're better off on board
Being ashore just don't feel right.

Stupendous

I had just imbibed a glass or three
Of a cut-price, cheap red wine
When I thought of the word 'stupor'
Even though I felt just fine.

Now stupor on its own just means
Tantamount to diddly squat
Put 'drunken' as a prefix
Helps explain it quite a lot.

The good thing about a stupor
In the morning it might seem
You can't recall the night before
Your memory's wiped quite clean.

It's halfway through the morning
When you face your first flashback
Of drunken dancing on the table
Being on stage and playing the sax.

Now the thing is when I'm sober
I can't play the saxophone
Or any other instrument
That's a fact that I bemoan.

I've left it much too late alas,
To be an accomplished player,
But I can practice drinking wine,
To me that sounds much fairer!

Witch Warning!

On a single point of order, I would just like to say,
Not all witches are bitches, even on a bad day,
The bad ones are black and the good ones are white,
And the ones that are white can be really contrite.

Now the black ones are horrid and can be awfully testy,
It takes just one spell to make you a wee beastie
Or a craw on a wa' by the side of a road
Or a newt on a chute or a slippery toad!

The white by contrast are all sweetness and light,
They're one in a million - but not terribly bright,
They're the ones that the Witch Finder burnt at the stake,
While the black ones had fun with a little sweepstake.

But there's one thing to know 'bout these women of Wiccan,
They can both be revengeful with one thing in common,
Upsetting them will lead to many regrets,
Their weird incantations are more than just threats!

So please play It safe, this advice may sound kitsch,
But be doubly sure when you encounter a witch,
Which spell comes your way is not your choice to pick,
So don't take the chance, compliment her broomstick!

First Pfizer/BioNTech coronavirus vaccinations take place in the UK

08 December 2020

They Think it's all Over

At last we've got a vaccine,
We might even have a cure,
Get our old lives back to normal,
No longer Lockdown to endure.

There's just one major stumbling block,
Well actually there's two,
There's a limited supply of it,
Might not get to me or you.

The other problem's bigger,
To do with storage and supply,
It has to stay well frozen
Or its effectiveness will die.

So what is the solution?
Health Practitioners are asking,
To vaccinate the masses,
Government ideas sadly lacking.

So it's lucky for the nation
That I have a cunning plan,
Let's throw a great big party,
Celebrate like a madman.

My idea if you will bear it,
Kills two birds with just one stone,
It's a sort of double whammy,
To the dog I've thrown a bone.

If we were to form a line-up
At the doctors' surgery,
Dance in syncopated rhythm,
Shuffle past all gleefully.

They could have the vaccination,
Primed and ready by the door,
As we dance a sort of Conga,
Wipe and stab – Virus no more.

So there it is quite simple,
Specialists don't complicate,
Just keep it simple stupid,
We've enough stuff on our plate.

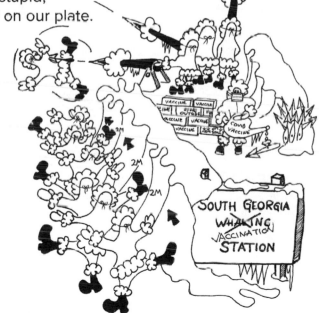

Don't Look so Down (It Could be Worse)

I effing fell the other day,
It's become more effing frequent,
I'm sorry for bad language,
It is so effing well indecent.

It's when I effing stand up,
From sitting in a chair,
And I take a small step forward,
And my effing leg's not there.

I'm sorry for my swearing,
I really must apologise,
But it is so damn frustrating,
I just hope you sympathise.

There I go with all that cursing,
My Mum would not be happy,
Wash my mouth with soap and water,
Carbolic soap tastes so damn crappy.

Getting back to the main story,
My wife doesn't know at all,
It's just before I go to bed,
When I mostly have my fall.

It's when I've been relaxing,
And I'm curled up on the sofa,
Get up, take one step forward,
And just end up falling over.

I thought there was a reason,
Could this be alcohol induced?
A cocktail of booze and Parkinson's,
Was the way falls were induced.

Now I'm not a biggish drinker,
Just one glass, perhaps another,
But my legs have always kept me up,
And I've never come a cropper.

On this latest trip however,
I was as sober as a Judge,
So my theory's out the window,
Parkinson's gave it a nudge.

So if you hear commotion,
My dear wife, in dead of night,
And I'm cursing like a docker,
I've fallen over, had a fright.

I'll tell you not to worry,
And go back to your sweet slumber,
I'll get the soap and water,
Wash my mouth out just for Mother!

Shirley Bassey

The News says Shirley Bassey's,
Got a new record on the way,
She's one hot, sassy lassie,
Is that girl from Tiger Bay.

She's still glamorous at eighty-four,
Even with her bingo wings,
She's really quite seductive,
Fans adore the songs she sings.

She started her career in clubs,
At just fourteen years of age,
She sang her little heart out,
Just a young girl, 'Centre Stage'.

But something made her sparkle,
Through tobacco smoke and grime,
Her performance monumental,
She has stood the test of time.

It was tough and really challenging,
Growing up in Tiger Bay,
It was part of Cardiff's docklands,
But she rose above the fray.

It may have been a poor place,
Badly bombed in World War Two
But like Bond's forever diamonds,
She shone bright, her craft she grew.

At the age of only nineteen years,
Helped by sultry sex appeal.
For the sum of fourteen pound a week,
She got her first big record deal.

Her very first recording,
'Burn My Candle' it was called,
Was banned by BBC stuffed shirts,
"Suggestive content", they're appalled.

Sadly seventy odd years later,
Her last album's on the way,
It's goodbye to ostrich feathers,
Sequinned ball gowns packed away.

She has had a great adventure,
Lavish shows and hits galore,
Has three Bond theme tunes to her name,
With Don Barry keeping score.

So thank you Shirley Bassey.
For your glittering career,
You've been married twice beforehand,
Want another? Well I'm here!

Celebrating Andrew

Andrew is Scotland's Patron Saint
And was the very first apostle
Now every year we celebrate
His life which was colossal.

He was in the family fishing boat
By the shores of Galilee
When Jesus Christ approached him
'Leave you nets and follow me'.

Andrew knew this was a special man
And immediately left the lake
To move from catching fish to men
Was the journey he would take.

Likewise, his brother Peter
Left the family straightaway
He was the rock on which was built
The kirk we know today.

Andrew served his master faithfully
And everywhere he went
He preached his Christian values
His time on earth well spent.

But the Romans didn't like that
They saw him as a threat
Ordered his execution
But he wasn't finished yet!

He felt he was unworthy
To die just like his Master
So a saltire cross he chose instead
Knowing death would not come faster.

For three long days he hung there
Still preaching 'til the end
Spreading his beliefs and values
Andrew's strong faith did not bend.

Let's all celebrate St Andrew's Day
With feasting, songs and verses
After all it was our patron saint
Who produced the loaves and fishes.

Celebrating Stan

St Andrew's Day is here again,
Other saints' days can be had,
But I much prefer the local boy,
I hope that don't sound bad.

To say he was a local lad
Is not entirely true.
He was one of Christ's Apostles,
Peter's brother, was Andrew.

I suppose the burning question is,
'Why the hell he's not a Scot?'.
He's a Red Sea postcode person
From a land that's baking hot.

So why's this foreign lad been picked
To represent our great country,
Instead of much more local saints,
Like Taffy Dave or wee Geordie?

The thing that's come as quite a shock,
Andrew's not just our wee patron,
Represents fishmongers, singers too,
And a wheen of other nations.

'So why the patron saint for Scots?'
I ask the same old question,
Was it 'cos he liked to drink Irn Bru.
Or his Mammy was Glaswegian?

No, not at all! If truth be told,
Scotland's young amongst the nations.
Not like her older neighbours,
Who'd received their allocations.

Of the few saints left to choose from,
Saint Andrew's name just clicked,
Because it matched the old Fife town,
This intrepid saint was picked.

Today his name is known worldwide,
University, golf course, flag and more.
Let's celebrate Saint Andrew,
'Bargain Buy' at the Super Saint Store!

Virally Yours

The virus has mutated,
What's that mean to you and me?
Spreading faster than a monkey swings
From tree to tree to tree.

This brand-new strain of virus,
Is so much easier to catch,
We'll have to stay indoors and hide,
Until this new strain's met its match.

If this carries on much longer,
We'll all have withered limbs,
There'll be future generations,
Who have never been to gyms.

And if there ever is vaccine,
You can forget about your Gran,
Delivery drivers get it first,
"Big it up" for the White Van Man.

They've kept the country going,
They're the rulers of the road,
They deliver food and parcels,
To the Virus, won't be bowed.

They've been handling loads of boxes,
Leaving parcels at your door,
They're the kings of all the byways,
Pressing the pedal to the floor.

If you're craving for some freedom,
Out and about not stuck indoors,
Work in parcel distribution,
Delivering stuff to people's doors.

Andrew Marr Show: New Covid strain 'out of control', says Hancock   20 December 2020

Where's Hancock?

Has anyone seen Matt Hancock,
Since the Andrew Marr news show?
He said the virus had mutated,
And was now out of control.

You can bet your bottom dollar,
That Boris was not best pleased,
When the Frenchies shut the borders,
'Cos he's run out of French cheese.

Now no-one's seen poor Matthew,
Since going into Number Ten,
The cameras haven't clicked and whirred,
'Cos he's not come out again.

He's been chained up in the basement,
In the style of Terry Waite,
Being taunted by the person,
The Civil Servants love to hate.

Priti Patel, the bully,
Looking not so pretty now,
Dressed up like a dominatrix,
Giving Matt an awful row.

What's to become of Hancock
Who made his colleagues frown,
'Cos he told the truth on TV?
He's just let the side right down.

You can tell great politicians,
Because all they do is lie,
You can see their lips are moving,
As they look you in the eye.

Now Hancock shouldn't get the blame,
'Cos he's made a daft mistake,
He don't deserve to disappear,
We're not in a Soviet State.

'You're as good as the tools you work with.'
The excuse bad workmen mutter,
There's loads of tools in Westminster,
Led by an utter nutter.

So Boris, let Matt Hancock go,
You can send him down to Dover,
He can alleviate the gridlock,
Let him be the truck controller.

Happy Covid Christmas

Happy Christmas everybody,
Time to rejoice and sing,
But what is there to sing about
With this Covid 19?

Nearly 60,000 passed away,
But one hundred years ago,
50 million met their maker,
As statisticians show.

Back in the nineteen hundreds,
When Spanish Flu was rife,
It really was a gamble,
If you lived or lost your life.

So if you're feeling upset,
That you're in a highish tier,
And you shouldn't mix your households,
Well there always is next year.

I know it sounds quite crass of me,
If your livelihood's at risk,
But so are your distant relatives,
Who could get the Covid kiss.

So goodbye aunts and uncles,
Oh and grandma please don't sob,
Didn't have to meet this Christmas,
And let the virus do its job.

Merry Christmas

It's Christmas season here again
Happens same time every year
But unlike all the others
Covid's ruined our festive cheer.

Let's not forget the meaning
Of what Christmas is about
It's not gifts and over eating
It's Christ's birthday without doubt.

He was only 33 years old
When he died upon the cross
But he changed the world forever
Showed the Romans who was boss.

And what about his mother Mary
You can bet that she was sad
But at least we now get Easter eggs
So it's turned out not too bad.

It's really not a hardship
Spending Christmas on your own
It's not as if we're all caught up
In a bombed out blitzed war zone.

We really should stop moaning
Put it into some perspective
The rules that have been put in place
Are meant to be protective.

So if you really get upset
And Covid's got your goat
It's not like the Titanic
At least we're still afloat.

Now there is one shred of good news
A vaccination's on its way
We'll put up with a little prick
Boris Johnson's here to stay!

Hermit

I am a lonely hermit,
On a Christmas shopping spree,
I left my cave one sunny day,
Now Covid has got me.

Bordering on Chaos

Santa didn't make it
I'm sure that I've been good
Perhaps with the pandemic
He just wasn't in the mood.

I've just turned on the telly
And it seems he's been detained
Since Mr Macron shut the border
Travel hasn't been the same.

He had to take a virus test
And join a whopping queue
But when they spotted Rudolf's nose
They refused to let him through.

Lufthansa saved the day again
And went on a bombing run
Dropped Satsumas down the chimney
Of every British home.

So Santa put your feet up
'Cos there'll always be next year
If the new strain hasn't wiped us out
And assuming we're still here!

NON!

It's Not a Game

We may well now have a vaccine,
The Covid bug to beat,
Let's not forget those gone before,
Nearly one in every street.

They say it's a game changer,
But who says that it's a game?
Over seventy thousand passed away,
Whose families won't be the same.

We see politicians beaming,
Saying that we're out of the woods,
But it's really down to scientists,
'Cos they came up with the goods.

So when we're out the tunnel,
As Boris did allude,
Let's invest in British science,
They're the ones who have done good.

As for the individual,
Who likened Covid to a game,
You really should take back your words,
And hang your head in shame.

Pandemic Petrol Pump Palaver

There's really no denying it,
Some people just are thick,
There's lots of different categories,
But this one was a flipping brick.

I'll set the scene first if I may,
There's frost lying on the ground,
It's the second week in January,
And New Strain Covid's all around.

I had gone to get some petrol,
Before my car runs dry and stops,
You'd never think we were in lockdown,
Seems everybody's at the shops.

I was at the lead-free petrol pump,
And I was filling up my car,
Looking at the people in the queue,
Looks like they'd come from near and far.

They were gathered by the doorway,
Social distancing forgotten,
And I'm standing thinking they're all fools,
It's more than petrol they'll be getting.

It was when I'd filled the car up,
Could it not get any worse?
As I joined what's vaguely termed a queue,
I let out a little curse.

This fat person just in front of me,
Who obviously doesn't feel the cold,
Let this sprightly granny push in front,
My face a picture to behold.

What made me think he's really dumb,
Was when he reached the sliding door,
He stood there right in front of it,
Separation rules ignored.

Now there's no exaggeration,
This idiot was fat,
And he completely blocked the sliding door,
There's no room to swing a cat.

The only way the granny could
Leave the shop and get outside,
Was to shimmy through the gap he'd made,
As he moved his bulk aside.

I suppose you'd call it justice,
For queue-jumping in my queue,
'Cos if the fat guy has got Covid,
Well now granny, so have you!

Communication Breakdown

My left leg and my right leg
Are both waiting patiently,
Instead of moving forward
I'm just stuck here like a tree,
My legs are standing waiting
For the message to be told,
But the signals they are lacking,
It's like my brain has been furloughed.

Meanwhile in the control room,
Upstairs inside my skull,
My brain is working overtime
With something neurological,
It's split right down the middle
On which foot to move off first,
And I'm left here in this doorway
Neither leg will be coerced.

Since it is a 50/50 split,
Let's put it to the test,
But the guys in the control room
Are as baffled as the rest,
Someone has nicked the Dopamine,
Has been doing it for years,
They think it's Mr Parkinson
Just one of many puppeteers.

Meanwhile my legs are now impatient
And they're raring just to go,
If they do not get a signal soon
A temper tantrum they will throw,
The left foot will take off at first
With the right foot close behind,
Seems the left foot never told the right,
Setting off at the same time.

That might be so, I'd like to know
Just where does that leave me?
Well, tripping up and falling down
As if on a pair of skis,
They'll think I'm drunk, which I am not,
I'm as sober as a judge,
My left foot tripped my right one
When my brain gave it a nudge.

It's all down to communication,
A thing my nervous system's lacking,
If I was manning the control room,
They'd be looking at a sacking,
To be fair it's really not their fault,
My neurons aren't to blame
It's my Parkinson's that should be sacked
But he clings on just the same.

Tremor Tantrums

It's bad news if you've got Parkinson's,
In lots of different ways,
But what occupation would be difficult,
If a bad tremor came your way?

I suppose if you're a Painter,
And your subject's sitting still,
Instead of a great portrait,
Call it abstract that's the drill.

Now a Decorator's not a Painter,
Unless you're Michelangelo,
If you specialise in ceilings,
Poor paint work is going to show.

What if you were a Conductor?
Not on a bus, not anymore,
But of a philharmonic orchestra,
Duff notes, you'll be shown the door!

If you're Ground Crew at an airport,
With those things like ping-pong bats,
Sending planes to wrong gate numbers,
Ground Controllers having spats.

Or an Army Major-General,
Pointing to a campaign map,
Sending troops in wrong directions,
Invade ourselves, 'There's a good chap!'

At least there's one thing that we're good at,
With our Parkinsonian shake,
We can always make great cocktails,
Let's celebrate for goodness sake!

PC Plod

I've just received a letter
An official one of course,
From our local law enforcement chap
In the new Scottish Police Force,
He wants help with his enquiries
Any information we would share,
After reading in the letter
On what sounds an unruly pair.

There's been criminal activity
Happening further down our street,
That awful type of low-life
That you would not wish to meet,
It seems that they turned out to be
Quite light upon their feet,
But the letter of the law mentioned
They'd been acting indiscreet.

It appears that our two suspects
Who have now gone on the run,
Had just burglarised a dwelling
Of an almost princely sum,
They used an old wheelbarrow
To transport what they were nicking,
To steal someone's wheelbarrow
Is so low and very sickening.

Do we have any security
Or video tapes to share,
And have we ever clapped our eyes
On this delinquent thieving pair?
To see someone push a wheelbarrow
In this neighbourhood is rare,
Seems even so the miscreants
Had vanished in thin air.

How do the local coppers
Plan to clap cuffs on these thieves?
Make the streets much safer places,
Protect us all from their misdeeds,
They've all been out and on patrol
Searching streets for the missing barrow,
We don't have security cameras yet
So no tapes for Plod to borrow.

Unless the Police Force budget cuts
Are a cut that's much too far,
And they mean that poor old PC Plod's
On patrol without a car,
His boots will surely wear out
As he's trailing round the street,
And since he's now on foot patrol
He'll cover a smaller beat.

At least now without their squad cars
Which they used when they patrolled,
All police will get much fitter,
A virtue that can only be extolled,
But what about the latest figures,
Their arrest and clean-up rate?
The statistics will no doubt reflect
They're in an awful state.

But statistically of course,
None of that will strictly matter,
The bottom line is our police
Will not be getting fatter,
The money they have saved
From buying enormous uniforms,
Will enable the Chief Constable
To renovate his holiday homes.

Instead of all that drama
And the screech of tortured tyres,
With blues and two's a blasting
From the roofs of their wee cars,
They're not hurtling down the road
In their jam sandwich giving chase,
It goes to show it's now become
A slow wheelbarrow race.

If the police are out there searching
For this pair of desperados,
They need a plan to catch them
As they race with their wheelbarrows,
What they need is some good teamwork
Like on sports day back at school,
A three-legged or a sack race
Or the dreaded egg and spoon.

It's a Date

Dedicated to the NHS and the Parkinson's Fife Team

I have just received a letter
With a date for my appointment
It was cancelled March last year
Which was such a disappointment.
The hospital was busy
It was putting up a fight
Because Covid was pandemic
We were in an awful plight.

But what about my Parkinson's
And how it's affected me
'Cos I haven't been to see
My specialist in neurology?
The last time that I saw him
Was almost twenty months ago
My symptoms have become much worse
As my motor movements show.

So I am really quite excited
To be seeing Dr Zeidler
Especially as I feel that
I am getting so much wobblier.
I'll find out if there's anything
That he can do for me
Maybe tweak my medication
Improve my life perceptively.

There is one little problem
Dr Z can't do his thing
He cannot, 'Ask the Audience'
'Phone a Friend', he cannot ring.
When I see him in his clinic
And he asks me how I am
I forget the things I want to say
'Cos I didn't write them down.

So this time when I see him
I'll be so much more prepared
And maybe he can help me
Because my symptoms I have shared.
I really do appreciate
What the NHS has done
They have bravely fought the virus
Let's hope their work is almost done.

Man Oh Man!

The Isle of Man has done it,
Covid clear for twenty days,
This means that they are virus free,
Oh what a joyful phrase!

So how did they achieve it?
Seems the authorities were bold,
They imposed a brutal lockdown,
And people did what they were told.

They closed all of their borders,
Which being an island was quite easy,
'Off Islanders' simply not allowed,
Apart from one chap on a jet ski!

The lockdown started straight away,
It began in March last year,
No one landed on the island,
Gates were padlocked on the pier.

But now they have their good news,
Their leaders weren't foolhardy,
If we had followed all their rules,
We could get out now and party.

So dear old British Government,
Have you learnt lessons from the Manx?
Were your restrictions really bold enough?
Don't look to us for thanks.

You opened up our borders,
To hordes of football fans,
And all that Boris told us,
Was to wash our sodding hands.

The quarantine rules are meaningless,
You can't work "Track and Trace",
Cumming's Barnard Castle trip,
Means he's completely in disgrace.

It wouldn't be so dreadful,
But we are an island too,
And instead of closing borders,
Uncle Cobley came right through.

Now we're the highest in the league,
But not in a sporting sense,
It's the people we've lost to Covid,
While Bo Jo's on the fence.

U-Turn Full Circle

We're in yet another lockdown
Due to the second or third wave
They're hoping that we'll ride it out
Surf the rip curl to be saved.

The thing that they don't realise
Have they not been on a beach?
Don't they know that there's a seventh wave?
Covid's biggest to unleash.

We're not out of the woods yet
Even with the vaccinations
Available to select groups
In GB's four home nations.

The PM's changed his mind again
Which just makes him sound gung-ho
Schools are now the virus hot spots
As any simpleton would know.

We won't be having Burns Night
Full blooded Scots will be appalled
That the haggis will not be addressed
Teuchter bands to be recalled.

Which is good news for the haggis
Won't be needed for the feast
Get to roam free for another year
On hills and glens released!

Dogged Determination

We've got a crossbreed Spaniel,
Alfie is his name,
And after this here lockdown,
He will never be the same.

He used to howl the house down,
The neighbours would complain,
While we were busy all at work,
He'd whinge without refrain.

But now we're social distancing,
He gets four walks a day,
There's three of us, we each take turns,
And one for luck we say.

We're in trouble when it's over,
And "new normal" has begun,
However will poor Alfie cope,
Isolated on his own?

Will I have to stay at home,
If he reverts to his old way,
It's awful when the neighbours moan,
About his howling every day.

I've stumbled on a cunning ruse,
For premature retirement,
What would you do? I hear you muse,
Dog sitting's the requirement.

Not Newsworthy

I am very disappointed,
I had my jab today,
It's supposed to fight the Covid,
Make Pandemic go away.

I thought that I'd be famous,
Filmed by all the TV crews,
But I wasn't even interviewed,
I'm not on the national news.

The amount of times I've seen it,
People getting their injections,
Surely everybody's getting filmed,
When they have their vaccinations.

I've got my second dose in May,
Perhaps I'll get filmed then,
But by that time I doubt it,
I'll never make the News at Ten.

What if at the vaccine centre,
Instead of giving them my arm,
I bared my naked bottom,
Would that have triggered the alarm?

The nurses would have called the cops,
And I would have been arrested,
My story would have caused a stir,
On news headlines I'd be pasted.

So that's what I will do in May,
To get me on the news at last,
But you know that you won't see my face,
You will only see my........

Thanks, I'm Off

I'm not great at making speeches
So I've writ this verse instead
From a bunch of jumbled up words
That were circling in my head.

I've finally made my mind up
On what I am going to do
It's not been an easy process
And I had to think it through.

It involves some other people
My children and my wife
But I have to do what's best for me
Give me quality of life.

The first cut is the deepest
As the well-known saying goes
You've got to get it just right
As every surgeon knows.

So I've come to a decision
It is time for me to go
And dedicate my days instead
My Parkinson's to slow.

Parkinson's is unforgiving
Affects your body and your mind
But a healthier existence
Slows the symptoms people find.

My Parkinson's won't kill me
Not just yet, you've got to know
One day I'll be 'body popping'
But there's ways to make it slow.

I'll spend my days with exercise
And contemplative meditation
Instead of dealing with some folk
Practiced in the art of masturbation.

Now, not everyone's a wanker
I have got to make that clear
But I've met an awful lot of them
In my glittering career.

I've also met some splendid folk
Who outweigh all the tossers
They made working here so worthwhile
But it's time to cut my losses.

So, I hope you all appreciate
I'll not leave you in the lurch
But I want to spend my time wisely
Before my coffin hits the dirt.

If you ever come on down my way
And you see me on my bike
Wind your window down, shout something rude
'Cos you know that's what I like.

I'll remember all the good old days
Suppose I'll mutter 'you're a wanker'
Who cares, it may be true or not,
I've set sail and raised my anchor.

So, it is with such a heavy heart
That I bid you all adieu
I'll remember you for always
No, that's not entirely true!

If you haven't had a whip-round
Not like me to save the day
You could always give to charity
It's called Parkinson's UK.

What is Parkinson's?

Parkinson's is a progressive neurological condition which gets worse over time and does not yet have a cure.

People with Parkinson's don't have enough of the chemical dopamine because some of the nerve cells that make it have died. Without it people can find that their movements become slower so it takes longer to do things.

Symptoms most commonly associated with Parkinson's are tremor and stiffness but there can also be over forty other symptoms, which affect each person individually.

Around 145,000 people live with Parkinson's in the UK and it's the fastest growing neurological condition in the world.

There are lots of different treatments, therapies and support available to help manage the condition. Parkinson's researchers are continuously working hard to develop new and better treatments - and one day a cure.

Poems In Alphabetical Order — Page Number